GUIDE FOR

ADOLESCENT TRANSITION

Smith Palma

Table of Contents

Chapter 1

INTRODUCTION

All facets of clinical medicine are practiced in the treatment of teenage patients against the backdrop of rapid changes in their physical, psychological, and social development.

Specific illness patterns, peculiar symptom presentations, and, most importantly, one-of-a-kind treatment and communication issues are the results of these modifications. Working with adolescents might be challenging as a result. However, practicing medicine with young people can be rewarding and successful with the correct abilities. Everyone who interacts with young people professionally needs these skills.

As a little child approaches puberty, their parents continue to bear the bulk of the responsibility for all facets of their health. By the conclusion of adolescence, the young person will be largely responsible for their own health difficulties.

In addition to adding communication and family participation to the regular adult consultation, taking an accurate history requires specialized professional communication skills that take into account new life domains that are not applicable to children (sex and drugs).

Adolescent physical exams necessitate special expertise, such as pubertal assessment, as well as respect of privacy and personal integrity. If doctors are to manage concerns of adherence (compliance), identification, consent and secrecy, as well as interactions between young people and their families, they must be knowledgeable about adolescent development. It is abundantly obvious from the results of randomized controlled trials that such skills can be learned and applied successfully in basic care.

What kind of development and growth should adolescents expect?

Your adolescent develops normally as they go through physical, mental, emotional, and social growth. Teenagers range in age from 10 to 20. Early (10 to 13 years old), Middle (14 to 17 years old), and Late (after 17 years old) are the three stages that make up this time period (18 to 20 years of age).

What changes in the body take place?

- The voice gets deeper for the male
- Body odor will start to appear.
- Acne might develop.

On some areas of your child's body, like the face and underarms, there will be growth of pubic hair.

During this time, boys grow 4 inches on average.

Girls gain 312 inches in height annually. Boys acquire 20 pounds on average every year. Girls acquire 18 pounds on average every year.

What social and emotional changes take place?

Your kid might start acting more independently. He or she might prioritize spending time with friends above family. As your child's responsibility grows, he or she can start to rely on themselves.

Your child might be affected by peer pressure and his or her friends.

He or she might experiment with activities like smoking, consuming alcohol, or engaging in sexual activity.

The interpersonal connections of your youngster will develop. He or she might develop the ability to put the needs of others before their own.

What mental modifications occur?

The way your youngster sees himself or herself will change. He or she will start to form their own personal principles, values, and ideals. He or she might discover new beliefs and contest established ones.

Your kid will get the ability to think in novel ways and comprehend intricate concepts. He or she will gain knowledge through focused, divided concentration. Your kid will learn to reason rationally, make wise decisions, and think abstractly.

The capacity for understanding and deriving meaning from symbols or images is known as abstract thinking.

Your youngster will grow in terms of self-image and future planning. Your child will choose who they want to be and what they want to do with their lives. Your child is now aware of the distinctions between objectives, fiction, and reality.

How can I support my teenager?

Establish clear guidelines and adhere to them. Set a positive example for your kids. Your youngster should be informed about sex, drugs, and alcohol.

Participate in your kid's activities. Keep in touch with his or her professors. Learn about their friends. Be there for him or her and spend time with them. Be aware of the early warning symptoms of drug use, depression, and eating disorders such bulimia or anorexia.

This may present an opportunity for you to assist your child before issues get out of hand.

Encourage healthy eating and daily exercise of at least one hour. Fruit, vegetables, and sources of protein including chicken, fish, and legumes are all part of a healthy diet. Eat fewer foods that are heavy in sugar and fat. Make sure he or she has breakfast so they can start the day with vigor.

Healthy Foods and child care

Your right to participate in planning for your child's care. Find out what's wrong with your child's health and how to treat it. With the help of your kid's medical professionals, go over treatment choices and determine what kind of care you want for your child. Only as a teaching tool is the information above intended. It is not meant to serve as medical advice for specific ailments or course of treatment.

Before beginning any medical regimen, check with your doctor, nurse, or pharmacist to ensure that it is both safe and beneficial for you.

Physical, behavioral, cognitive, and emotional growth and change are all a part of the lifetime process known as human development. Huge changes occur throughout the early phases of life, from infancy to childhood, childhood to adolescence, and adolescent to maturity. Each person grows attitudes and values throughout the process that influence decisions, connections, and comprehension. Additionally, a lifelong process is sexuality.

Sexual beings include newborns, kids, teenagers, and adults. Laying the groundwork for a child's sexual development is just as crucial as supporting their physical, emotional, and cognitive development. It is the obligation of adults to assist youngsters in understanding and accepting their changing sexuality.

Specific indicators are present at each developmental stage. For most kids in this age range, the developmental criteria listed below are applicable. However, because every child is unique, they could progress through these stages sooner or later than other kids their age.

Parents or other caregivers should speak with a doctor or other child development specialist whenever they have questions regarding the development of a particular kid. The terms "males," "females," "boys," and "girls" refer to people who are biologically allocated to the male or female sex and have the accompanying body parts, regardless of how they identify with their gender.

Chapter 2

DIFFERENT AREAS OF DEVELOPMENT

Developmental task

Young people will navigate puberty and the end of their growth during adolescence. They will also acquire sexually dimorphic body shapes, new cognitive abilities, a clearer sense of their personal and sexual identities, and a certain amount of emotional, personal, and financial independence from their parents.

It is becoming more well acknowledged that adolescence presents unique difficulties for the prevention and treatment of disease.

This dynamic backdrop of growth must be considered in all clinical encounters with adolescents. When comparing a 13-year-old boy in very early puberty with underdeveloped abstract thinking to a 16-year-old female who is sexually mature, at her final height, and has well-developed adult cognitive skills, issues around the care of chronic sickness, for instance, can be extremely different.

Psychosocial development

Adolescence begins with bodily changes, but it also brings about psychological and social changes that make this time a crucial step toward adulthood. Adolescence has been positioned in a range of models or theories that encompass human development from conception to death. The majority of these are "stage" models, where each step must be finished before moving on to the next.

Different "tasks" are identified by each concept as constituting adolescence. Some school of thought dwelled on various developmental areas. Some were particularly interested in the development of the psychosexual, viewing adolescence as a recapitulation of the emergence of sexual consciousness in infancy. Some concentrated on cognitive growth, believing that the emergence of the capacity for abstract thought would enable the shift to independent adult functioning. The difficulties surrounding the formation of one's own identity have most recently been recognized by a different school of thought as being essential to the concept of adolescence. The biopsychosocial model is a more practical one since it recognizes the biology (puberty and sexual development) as well as psychological and social aspects of adolescence.

Challenges

Many of the models used to describe the teenage stage have come under fire for not explicitly recognizing that the young person is a part of a "system." Their place in the system is determined by their interactions with other system components, which are influenced by both internal and external needs (or tasks).

External or societal changes interact with internal physical and psychological changes.

The accomplishment and negotiation of the various tasks are so interrelated and dependent upon one another taking place at the proper moment. When these issues are combined with health or illness, they create special management and communication problems, especially when it comes to risk-taking behaviors and adherence to prescribed treatments or medical advice.

Psychological Alterations

Young people gradually start to develop abstract thinking in their early adolescence, which is the capacity to represent reality with internal symbols or images. In contrast to the more simplistic concrete thinking, where items must stand in for "things" or "ideas" in order to solve problems, abstract thinking helps us to consider potential outcomes and think speculatively about the future.

Knowing whether a young person has a limited or well-developed capacity for abstract thought is important since it will determine whether they can offer informed consent to treatment and independently manage their chronic illness regimens.

Recognizing how psychological changes interact with puberty is crucial, especially in the context of a developing sense of sexuality and body image. Body image and self-esteem are susceptible to physical consequences of chronic illnesses as well as variations in peers' timing of puberty.

Social evolution

Typically, adolescence is characterized as a time of gaining independence. However, it is more correct to refer to a shift in the ratio of the young person's system's dependency and independence (parents, peers, community, and even health professionals). The young person's surroundings, including the various social and cultural expectations, determines when these changes will occur.

While puberty and cognitive development are mostly influenced by biology, environmental and sociocultural factors play a larger role in psychological and social development. The social and psychological realms may be severely condensed in non-Western civilizations.

Although recalling our youth with accuracy can be challenging, most people don't forget their adolescent.

Adolescents transition from a position where they define themselves in reference to others to one where they define other people in respect to themselves. This manner of viewing oneself makes it challenging to comprehend how one's behavior affects other people or to be concerned about how one's behavior might influence others. The value of information that has been "passed down" by adults is low. Teenagers could also fervently believe that no one else can truly get how a teenager feels.

Physical Improvement

Rapid physical change, such as puberty, the pubertal growth spurt, and associated maturational changes in other organ systems, provide as a backdrop for psychological development. Tanner phases) are stages in the development of secondary sex traits that both boys and girls go through.

You can measure testicular development with the Prader orchidometer: 1-3 ml for prepubescence, 4 ml for beginning puberty, 8 ml to 10 ml for mid-puberty, and 15 ml to 25 ml for complete puberty.

Prepubescence to full reproductive potential can develop in as short as 18 months or as long as 5 years. Boys can express the full spectrum at the age of 13. The earliest evidence of puberty in boys (growing testicular volume) starts at a mean age of 12 years, barely six months after girls produce breast buds (the first sign of puberty), despite the fact that girls appear to undergo puberty much earlier than boys do.

Due to the female growth spurt occurring earlier in puberty (mean age 11–12 years) than it does in boys, who experience it later in puberty, girls also appear to be significantly more developed earlier (mean age 14 years).

Menarche is the pivotal moment in a girl's adolescence. In most developed nations, the average age at menarche decreased significantly throughout the first half of the 20th century before stabilizing in the 1960s at roughly 13 years for white girls and 12.5 years for black girls.

Delay in puberty and small stature, especially in males, are the most prevalent clinical problems about puberty. The 97th centile for growing larger testicles (>4 ml) is 14 years old. So, at the age of 14–15, 2% of males will still be prepubertal (and therefore small).

Although it is nearly always a normal variety (constitutional delay of puberty and growth), which is frequently family, this can be extremely upsetting. Most boys will already be showing early symptoms of testicular enlargement by the time they visit their doctor, which can be determined using an orchidometer.

It is safe to assume that puberty has started for males above the age of 15 with testicular volumes of 4 ml or higher. A Pediatric Endocrinologist should be consulted for additional research if a person is 15 years old and has not yet shown any signs of puberty.

Chapter 3

EARLY PUBERTY AND DELAYED PUBERTY

The interval between childhood and adulthood is known as adolescence. It involves some significant adjustments to the body as well as how a young person interacts with the outside environment.

Children and their families may experience anticipation and worry as a result of the numerous physical, sexual, cognitive, social, and emotional changes that take place during this period. Knowing what to anticipate at various junctures can help adolescents and young adults develop healthily.

Early adolescence (Ages 10 to 13)

Children frequently start to grow more swiftly during this stage. They also start to notice other physical changes, such as hair growth near the genitalia and under the arms, female breast development, and male testicular enlargement. It can be typical for some changes to begin as early as age 8 for females and age 9 for males. They often start a year or two earlier in girls than boys. On average 2-3 years following the beginning of breast development, many girls may begin their period around the age of 12.

Some people may be curious about and anxious about these physical changes, especially if they don't know what to expect or what is typical. At this time, some kids could also doubt their gender identification, and the beginning of puberty can be challenging for transgender kids.

Adolescents in their early years think in concrete, binary terms. There is little place for middle ground; everything is either fantastic or dreadful. It is common for adolescents to focus on themselves at this era (called "egocentrism"). As a result of this, preteens and young teenagers frequently feel self-conscious about their appearance and that their classmates are constantly evaluating them.

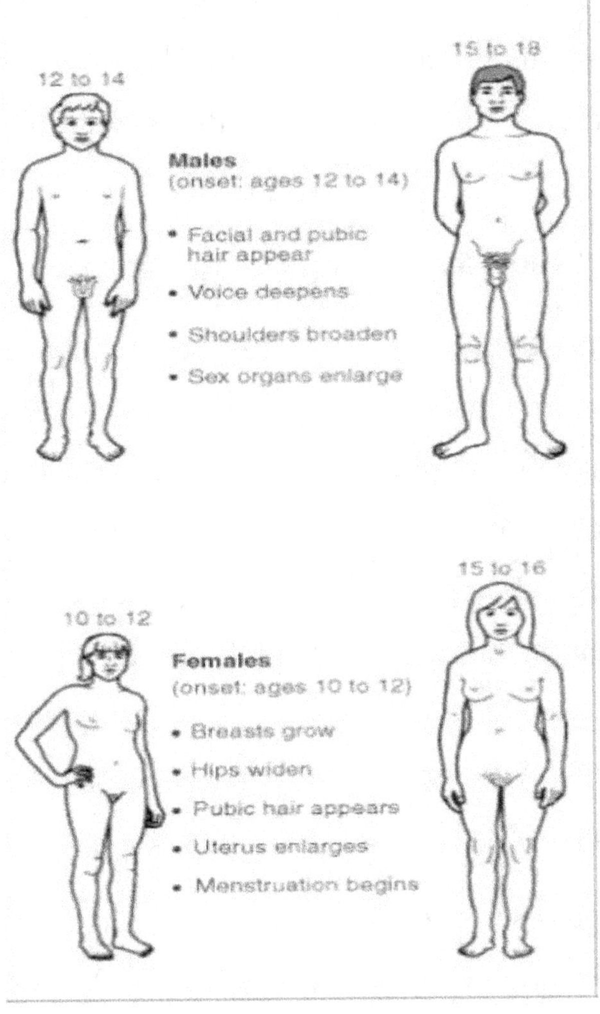

Preteens have more demands for privacy. They might begin to look for ways they can live independently of their family. They might test the limits during this process, and they might become upset if their parents or guardians enforce limitations.

Middle aged adolescence (Ages 14 to 17)

During middle adolescence, the body continues to change as it did during puberty. The growth spurt for the majority of guys will have begun, and puberty-related changes continue. As their voices become lower, they could experience some voice crackling, for instance. Some people get acne. For females, physical changes may be almost complete, and the majority of girls now experience regular menstruation.

Many teenagers start to show interest in romantic and sexual interactions at this age. If they do not have support from their friends, family, or community, it may be stressful for them to question and explore their sexual identity. Self-stimulation, often known as masturbation, is another common approach for adolescents of all genders to explore sex and sexuality.

As they try to gain greater independence, many middle schoolers argue more with their parents. They might spend more time with friends and less time with relatives. At this age, peer pressure may be at its highest and they are quite self-conscious.

Even though the brain is continuously developing and changing at this era, a typical middle teenager nevertheless thinks very differently from an adult. The frontal lobes are the last parts of the brain to grow, and it takes a person until they are well into their 20s for this process to be finished. The coordination of complicated decision-making, impulse control, and the capacity to weigh various options and implications are all greatly influenced by the frontal lobes.

Middle schoolers have a greater capacity for abstract thought and "the big picture," but they may not have the practical application skills to use it.

Outside of these circumstances, they might be able to reason through the logic of avoiding dangers, but when impulses are involved, intense emotions frequently still influence their decisions.

Late adolescence 18 to 21-year-olds and older

Late teens typically have reached their full adult height and have finished their physical development. By this point, they often have more self-control and may be better equipped to weigh risks and rewards.

Teenagers transitioning into their early adult years now have a deeper feeling of their own uniqueness and can recognize their own beliefs. They might start to think more about the future and make choices based on their ideas and aspirations.

The stability of romantic and platonic relationships increases. Their emotional and physical distance from their family grows. However, many people restore a "adult" relationship with their parents, viewing them less as an authority figure and more as a peer with whom to discuss adult issues.

Adolescents' feeling of individuality interacts with the development of abstract thinking to produce awareness of outcomes for others but a belief in personal invulnerability—being "bullet proof." This idea might cause young individuals to take significant risks in terms of substance abuse, personal safety, or treatment compliance because they think that unfavorable consequences won't affect them.

Chapter 4

INTERACTING WITH TEENAGERS

Many teenagers and health experts believe that communication between children and doctors might be quite difficult. Only when working with children do doctors interact directly with adults in clinical practice.

Adult clinicians interact with other adults who, despite cultural differences, have societal norms and attitudes regarding health that are substantially similar to their own. Pediatricians negotiate treatment choices with parents, enlisting the children's input through explanation and parental authority.

In contrast, communicating with a personality undergoing rapid psychological and social change during a consultation with an adolescent can be difficult because they might not share an adult's understanding of society or adult cognitive abilities to weigh treatment options in light of potential health risks in the future. This difficulty is exacerbated by the various "young cultures" that coexist in our society, which is becoming more multicultural and racially varied.

Teenagers' average consultation periods with family doctors are lower than those of children or adults, according to general practice surveys, and many doctors are uncomfortable treating them. Fortunately, by receiving training in teenage development and adolescent health issues, clinicians can enhance their clinical and communication abilities with adolescents.

Parents: Tips: Journey Through Adolescence

When a child enters adolescence, both their parents and they frequently struggle with the shifting dynamics of the family. However, parents continue to be a vital source of support at this time.

You can take the following actions:

Aid your youngster in anticipating physical changes. Learn about puberty and what to expect. They should be reassured that bodily changes and developing sexuality are a natural and healthy component of growth. Allow youngsters to ask inquiries at their own pace and leave space for them. Consult your child's pediatrician as needed!

Start early-morning discussions of other crucial subjects. Keep lines of communication open regarding safe relationships, sex, sexuality, consent, and other topics (such as how to prevent sexually transmitted infection and pregnancy, and substance use). Starting these dialogues in the early stages of adolescence will help provide a solid foundation for discussions in the future.

Talk positively to your youngster at all times. Declare your advantages. Celebrate achievements.

Be encouraging, set boundaries, and have high expectations that are still acceptable. Set clear, realistic expectations for things like curfews, school participation, media consumption, and behavior.

Expand possibilities for greater independence over time as your youngster learns to accept responsibility. It has been demonstrated that children whose parents strive for this balance have lower rates of depression and drug use.

Discuss dangerous activities and their effects, such as substance abuse and sexual activity. Make certain that you lead by example. This can assist teenagers in thinking through or practicing decision-making in advance and preparing for when problems come.

Respect individuality and independence. All of this is a component of becoming an early adult. Always let your youngster know you are available to assist when necessary.

Teenage years might resemble being on a roller coaster. Your family can (attempt to) enjoy the ride by preserving strong and polite parent-child ties during this time!

Chapter 5

SUPPORTING YOUR TEENAGER

- How to Support Your teenager.
- Safeguarding their interest
- When to be worried

While many teenagers are excited about life after high school, others could be nervous about starting their adult lives. Even parents or other caregivers could feel anxious and stressed as their child gets closer to turning 17.

You might, for instance, ponder whether you have imparted to your adolescent all the knowledge necessary for them to grow into responsible adults. To ensure that they are ready for the real world, it certainly helps to take into account their development and provide them with the appropriate support.

You can learn more about what to anticipate from your teen's development in the sections below. You may learn about your teen's cognitive, physical, social, and emotional development. We also offer advice on how to keep your teen safe at this age as well as how to help them learn and grow.

Chapter 6

CHILD DEVELOPMENTAL MILESTONES

Language and Cognitive Milestones for teens

Most teenagers are well-organized by the time they turn 17 years old. They can so successfully balance their extracurricular interests, part-time jobs, and academic obligations. Although many 17-year-olds believe they are adults, their brains have not yet reached complete maturity. As a result, while having the ability to control their urges, they occasionally exhibit irresponsible behavior.

By this age, the majority of teenagers are also considering their future and may begin to make more specific plans for what they want to do after high school, whether it be plans for college, a job, or the military.

Around this time, fluid intelligence is also attained, which means 17-year-olds are better able to handle novel events and issues.

According to another school of thought, "They are leaning toward more formal operational thinking." They may also consider how others view them or how they feel about them, which is known as metacognition.

The majority of 17-year-olds are able to communicate on an adult level. They are not permitted to speak up or ask for explanation if they do not comprehend a word or phrase, nevertheless.

Teenagers frequently use slang, which may be more meaningful than formal language at this age.

Some 17-year-olds still find it challenging to comprehend double negatives, though. Although their attention spans have increased, it's still normal for children to get lost in lengthy, difficult inquiries.

- Added Cognitive Developments
- Able to speak in adult-like language
- Frequent use slang terms
- Deal better with difficulties, solves problems better than previous times in the past.
- Physical Development

By the time they become 17, most boys and females are completely formed. They have grown to their full height and are done with puberty. Males may, however, continue to grow physically, particularly if they start out later in life.

Even if they don't grow taller, most men and women will continue to gain weight.

In males, voices may continue to get deeper, and they may also develop more face and underarm hair.

At this age, teens frequently struggle with body image concerns since some don't like the physical changes they've gone through.

Acne can also spread widely.

Metabolism begins to slow down as they approach late puberty. Slows down to more adult ranges, making irregular eating more difficult at this age. Establish healthy sleeping, eating, and exercise routines so that when kids finish playing high school sports, they will still have a personal wellness plan.

Additional Physcial Changes

Full height is attained.

Males may still be developing their muscles after they have finished puberty.

Emotional and Social Milestones

For many teenagers, turning 17 marks an interesting turning point in their lives. Some of them start off on a straightforward path to adulthood. They take on more responsibility as time goes on and are ready to become independent.

Others, on the other hand, could be less sure of themselves as they approach adulthood. They might even feel disoriented and uncertain about the future. Teenagers at this age may also find it difficult to demonstrate responsibility with regard to their homework, housework, and everyday obligations and may worry about growing up.

Let your adolescent know that making errors is acceptable, Actually, you want people to make errors that are neither fatal or disastrous. Asking them what they learnt from their error or poor decision can help you avoid being a helicopter parent or a snowplow instead.

A 17-year-mood is generally calmer than they were during earlier adolescence. Less hormonal fluctuation and a greater sense of control are to blame for this. Teenagers may still experience emotional difficulties when they are faced with significant problems, though. Many are facing adult-sized issues for the first time, whether it be a broken heart or a college rejection letter.

When issues arise, parents are advised to dispute their teen's automatic views if they use absolutes like "ABC always happens" or "XYZ never happens." "These statements are rarely accurate in the real world. As a last resort, if they are unable to recall a period when that was not the case, ask them to envision it and describe how it could feel or appear. Ask them what measures they need to take to make that a reality after that."

Most teenagers are motivated by goals. They are starting to envision the kind of life they want to build after high school.

Make sure you are giving them room to discover their identity and what they want to do.

A lot of teens establish lasting connections. They form intimate bonds and are less prone to switch between cliques as a result. They learn the value of dependability as well. They desire to keep their promises when they make them to their pals.

When at home, your teen may choose to be alone in their room and spend the most of their spare time with friends.

At this age, the parent-teen connection may also change a little. As kids get more independent, that may mean growing apart from their parents for some people, while it may mean becoming closer to them as their drive to rebel wears off for others.

Developments in Social and Emotional Functioning

This milestone demonstrates greater autonomy from your parents.

Possess a greater capacity for forming more profound connections.

- Seek for intimacy.
- Desire adult leadership positions.
- Able to take action on pledges made.
- Other Significant Developments for Your Teenager.

Teenagers at the age of seventeen could be going through a number of firsts. Some of them, if they don't already have one, are getting their licenses and, in some cases, purchasing vehicles. While some people may be participating in hazardous activities, others are acquiring part-time work. Some might even be testing out unprotected sex, alcohol, or illicit substances.

And for some teenagers, their first meaningful romantic relationship—and possibly their first heartbreak—begins at age 17.

Additionally, keep an eye out for harmful dating situations, such as teen dating violence. Many teenagers find it difficult to handle these adult-like concerns.

Chapter 7

HELPING YOUR TEEN LEARN AND GROW

Encourage your teen to avoid obsessing on their appearance and instead concentrate on making healthy decisions like eating a balanced diet and exercising.

You should also advise against dieting or gaining weight. More than 50% of high school females are dieting and are worried about their weight. Additionally, you should do all of your effort to encourage your teen's autonomy and independence.

Just a few stages toward being an independent adult are letting your teen drive a car, acquire a job, and spend the night at home alone. However, it's also crucial to control them, particularly if they are making poor decisions or taking unwarranted risks.

Parents ought to gradually assign more responsibility as a result. Make sure they are familiar with how to use the kitchen, how often to wash the towels and bedding, and how to handle their funds. You don't want them to enter college with no knowledge of their credit standing.

Additionally, you should lay out specific guidelines for dating and frequently discuss consent, healthy relationships, and safe sex. You can also inspire your adolescent to pursue their interests and pastimes. Also, try your best to encourage your 17-year-old to read for pleasure. Teens' writing abilities and vocabularies both benefit from reading.

Safeguarding Your Teen

The top safety concerns for children this age continue to be substance misuse, safe driving, sexual activity, and mental health difficulties. In fact, a survey by the Centers for Disease Control and Prevention found that nearly 180,000 babies were born to teenagers between the ages of 15 and 19 and that 38% of high school students had sex while still in high school.

In addition, the survey found that over 20 million new STD cases among young people aged 15 to 24 were reported. Many teenagers of this age are sexually active. Be mindful of their sexual demands and keep in mind that they might require medical attention.

Make sure you discuss the value of consent as well as safe sex with your kid if you have any reason to believe that they are sexually active.

You could also want to give them some dating safety advice and talk to them about birth control.

Additionally, you should inquire about how they are feeling emotionally and mentally. Ask your teen open-ended inquiries and pay attention to what they have to say.

Once in a while make sure you have constructive dialogues about their increasing independence. Additionally, you need to monitor their security and well-being. Look for indications of despair and anxiety, as well as pay attention to their mood, self-care, sleeping patterns, and eating habits.

When to Be Worried

You are not alone if the idea of releasing your 17-year-old into the real world in the upcoming year concerns you. Many parents find it difficult to envisage their kid surviving in the adult world on their own. But between the ages of 17 and 18, there is frequently a lot of growth.

Teenagers also grow prepared to enter college, the military, or the workforce within that year.

You may wish to speak with a healthcare professional if your teen appears particularly unprepared for the responsibilities of adulthood. If your teen's mood or conduct undergoes significant changes, you should be concerned as well. One or more signs, such as a drop-in grade, changes in sleep patterns, or changes in weight or hunger, may point to a mental health condition or another underlying issue.

Contact the Substance Abuse and Mental Health Services Administration (SAMHSA) National Helpline at 1-800-662-4357 if your teen is suffering from anxiety or depression to learn more about treatment centers and other local support services.

Chapter 8

FACTORS AFFECTING THE ADOLESCENT AGE

Generational Difference:

The teenager is the one who is most impacted by the generation gap. The teenager, who resides in the peerage business, stands in for a society that is transitioning and changing. These are the changes that the developed adult society cannot acknowledge; rather, it would be condemning the creation of such a society.

The adolescent is still too immature to have a distinct personality and be able to express his opinions or attitudes. The adult culture has consistently disregarded the opinions and ideas of teenagers, resulting in a fight between an existing society and a society trying to form.

Adolescence is the worst victim of this conflict. He or she will always need to maintain a state of tension in order to get their own way when it comes to the style of their clothing, their hair, their speaking and acting according to their own beliefs and convictions. The conflict between adolescents and the established adult culture appears to highlight the generational divide.

They are demonstrations of how teenagers gradually stop being "parent-oriented" and start being "peer-oriented," which leads to conflict between the adult and adolescent societies. Due to the peer group's powerful influence, it sometimes happens that adolescents who walk away become drug addicts and lack morals.

The world is rapidly evolving, and the flood of knowledge brought on by the current supercomputer era is so perplexing to the older generation that they are unable to comprehend why teens think and act the way they do.

Adolescents must fight hard to develop their identities because authority in society is held by adults. In some circumstances, the information and abilities of the adult generation are rendered useless by those of the younger generation, and the adults are unable to gain the critical knowledge of the present while also learning how to use new technologies.

Due to this, the generation divide makes things harder for the teens.

Emotional instability:

Adolescence is a difficult time due of emotional instability as well. As one quickly approaches the peak of their physical, mental, and emotional growth, they must also go through a time of rapid transformation.

Fast physical changes, as well as rapidly developing mental skills and self-awareness, can make people anxious because they find it difficult to adjust to so many changes, as well as because they are aware of new issues and responsibilities that the adult generation wants them to take on even though they are not yet considered mature enough to do so.

It becomes very difficult to control the flow and bursting of emotions due to excess sex and other hormones.

The teenager is extremely easily angered and becomes agitated due to physiologic changes, particularly menstruation or ejaculation. The boy or girl is now cognitively well developed; he or she can better understand their circumstances, is more aware of the issues that lie ahead, and is mature enough to consider their careers as well.

Due to everything mentioned, the adolescent is anxious. Adolescence is a time of growth in all areas, yet emotionally, a person experiences weakness such as instability, rashness, and occasionally recklessness.

An adolescent is typically very sensitive and emotional. Because of the ups and downs in his emotions, he occasionally becomes anxious. He is becoming more self-conscious, and when he perceives that he has been harmed, he loses control. He may either become very upset or worried when he perceives that everything is working against him.

The adolescent should be handled sensitively and with sympathy.

It is undoubtedly a time of extremes; when things go well, when he succeeds and is recognized for his efforts and value, he feels incredibly ecstatic; nevertheless, when things go wrong, he may feel incredibly despondent. His actions show a lack of tolerance and patience. Adolescent has to learn lessons about moderation and temperance, two traits that they typically lack.

The temperamental health of the adolescent may be distorted by a rigid approach taken to quell the bursting of their emotions. In many cases, it was discovered that too rigid fathers were to blame for spoiling their kids, who later turned rebellious as they approached adolescence or adulthood. The teenager should be given the proper amount of freedom to work and think, lest this stunt his or her growth.

In a reviewed study of 2,000 kids, it was discovered that girls were indeed more sensitive than guys.

Even though this is the age when some people even attempt suicide, occasionally both of them get incredibly anxious. Adolescents are typically very ambitious people who dream of being great (sometimes imitating their role models). When obstacles repeatedly derail their aspirations, they become dissatisfied.

They are claims that excessive self-consciousness, an unusual state of inferiority complex, strained parent-child relationships, occasionally a repugnant attitude toward religion and growing repugnant to its tenets, getting apprehensive and harboring a sense of hatred at the initial experience of sex, or the social evils which he or she still considers himself or herself quite powerless to do anything about, were the main causes of the mental trouble of his subjects.

When there are no opportunities for self-expression, which the adolescent is so eager for, he or she also feels unsettled.

Only one-fifth of the teens claimed on the questionnaire that they frequently felt unhappy or depressed, yet nearly half of the subjects were experiencing terrible feelings, even if a much smaller proportion really appeared sad during interviews. Even while there was some degree of internal unrest, severe clinical depression was uncommon.

Adolescent turbulence is a fact, not a fiction, but its significance in terms of mental health has likely been overstated in the past.

Career Awareness

As one approaches adulthood in the latter years of adolescence, one begins to worry about their career. The chosen career is taken into consideration when choosing the courses and subjects.

Before becoming an adult, the adolescent reaches the adult level of cognitive development.

Due to this growth, a teenager knows where the best opportunities for a successful job are and how to best prepare for one.

The fact that the adolescent may not have acquired that degree of professional awareness in certain situations makes the parents uneasy, and they continue to nag their kids to work hard and consistently toward the desired vocation.

The adolescent may feel stressed out by the circumstance. However, while being unemployed for a brief period of time may not necessarily have a negative impact, it can raise anxiety. Those who must leave school early due to financial strain or another family issue would understandably be upset if they were unable to find employment.

When young people reach the age at which they are employable and, despite their best efforts, are unable to find employment, it affects their self-esteem and gives them a negative stigma.

Due to how severe the unemployment crisis is, the problem does not only begin when a person reaches the age of work but also when they are still students and begin to be concerned about it. Some dishonest persons in our culture would even consider defrauding such children by promising them wonderful jobs.

Relating with Adolescents

Adolescence is a crucial time since it marks a period of rapid and extensive physical, mental, and emotional growth. A child develops into a full adult via adolescence. However, as was mentioned before, it is a time of storm and tension.

Consequently, treating the adolescent requires being very thoughtful and sympathetic.

This most creative time in a person's life can be ruined by a hard treatment that is unaware of the developmental nature of adolescence and the requirements of the adolescent. Here are some recommendations for what should be done with regard to adolescents so that this time can genuinely serve as a pathway for guiding a child to the stage of a healthy maturity.

Physical Exercise

There is a growth spurt in the body. Adolescents are predisposed to participate in a wide variety of physical activities. He or she may join a gym, sports club, or like playing a game that is made available to them depending on their peer group and home setting. For the teenagers' optimal physical development, physical education lessons are taught on a regular basis in a decent school.

Games and physical activities should be varied enough to suit the children's ages, physical characteristics, and gender. They ought to be made in a way that kids can enjoy them wholeheartedly and with great pleasure. If the adolescent is not given a conducive atmosphere in this regard, it will harm them physically and, inadvertently, mentally and emotionally.

It makes sense that an energetic adolescent would want to make a statement so that others would be drawn to him. If his guardians do not care about the company that their ward is keeping, he may go astray and become a delinquent and a criminal as well if no opportunities for appropriate activities are accessible to him.

Physical activities are a good way to channel soaring sexual cravings in order to prevent the innocent adolescent from ruining themselves when pubescence begins.

Physical activity is important for two reasons: first, it is the best time in life to grow a well-built, muscular body through adequate physical activity; and second, it allows you to creatively use your youthful energy for physical development.

If this time is used effectively, individuals may develop into exceptional athletes, athletes, gymnasts, swimmers, shooters, and others. On the other hand, if this time is spent without making any physical efforts, eventual success won't be as high as intended.

There are various activities available, including hiking, mountaineering, and Yogasana (boy scouts and girl guides). The adolescent should be given the opportunity to try one or more of these activities and grow to fully like it. Such actions stimulate, sublimate, and develop the surroundings.

Emotional Sublimation:

Adolescence is a time when emotions such as joy, grief, anxiety, frustration, love, and wrath can be felt strongly.

They have the power to either do or undo. If the energy created by these emotions is used in a constructive manner, life will progress as intended; nevertheless, if the emotions are allowed to run wild in an environment with no constructive programs at all, they will show themselves to be powerful forces that can destroy life.

A teenager might wish to engage in activities like music, sketching and painting, collecting artifacts, reciting and writing poetry or stories, or expressing oneself in one literary or artistic medium or another. These activities would give the adolescents' strong emotions a conduit to be sublimated.

These are the activities that control emotions and focus their energy for greater personality development. Any person whose emotions have not been tamed by literary and artistic endeavors or some other social service program cannot be ethically good. Sports and games also aid in emotional growth.

Students can receive emotional training through acting in plays where emotions are conveyed in ways that have positive effects on both the actors and the audience. When emotions are used for literary and artistic endeavors, they are beneficial for development.

Parents should support their children in engaging in these pursuits. A suitable setting must be offered for the pursuit of the same. Additionally, schools should encourage and direct their students to pursue their interests in the arts and literature.

Allow teenagers to choose from a wide variety of activities for their hobbies. Let there be clubs for people who enjoy photography or computer-based activities, for example. Along with developing their knowledge in various subjects, the pupils' emotions will also be sublimated.

Excellent Literature:

During adolescence, reading interest increases significantly. The people in the household and the school teachers should further foster this passion. One's academic development would be hampered if they did not take an interest in reading throughout this time.

Only such students have the potential to develop into eminent, passionate readers. But just as crucial is the advice that kids should only read good books, whose ideas and sentiments they may utilize to shape their developing and extremely impressionable minds.

Particularly during the pubescent stage, youngsters are more prone to be drawn to reading pornographic books. It is the responsibility of both parents and teachers to ensure that children of this age may easily access engaging and practical material that is appropriate for their mental development.

These publications can be of many different genres, including poetry, novels, dramas, picture books, illustrated tales, biographies, books about travel and daring exploits, whether real or imagined. The children's natural curiosity ought to be satiated in full.

Books on history, science, geography, and other topics should be made available as well, depending on the interests of the kids. Every school needs a strong library as well as a comfortable reading area with a variety of materials.

Socialization:

When we read Piaget's theory of cognitive development, we get the impression that social viewpoint is not given the credit it deserves because Piaget believes that the process of development is primarily driven by biological maturity and is focused on the individual kid.

With relation to tasks that have social relevance, Margaret Donaldson and her colleagues showed how the child's ability to consider others' viewpoints grows with age. This demonstrates each child's social growth, which is crucial for cognitive development as well. Piaget never recognized the value of socialization from this perspective.

The years of adolescence, in Piaget's view, are when a person reaches the pinnacle degree of cognitive development; socialization has a significant role to play in helping people reach this stage.

Therefore, it is the responsibility of the parents and teachers to ensure that the developing child has access to a very suitable social environment where he can engage in a variety of activities that provide opportunities for rich interactions. The social environment of an individual has a strong positive association with their cognitive and moral growth.

The transition into a group of friends that is constantly expanding occurs during adolescence. His peerage was first limited to a small number of his classmates, but with time, he began to interact with students outside of his class and form friendships with many of them.

While participating in curricular and extracurricular activities like games, sports, scouting, outings, trips or tours, picnics, etc., students get to know one another. An adolescent develops a strong desire to travel with his friends. Their numbers are rising quickly. An adolescent might enjoy joining a variety of clubs.

The teenager becomes quite social as a result of all of this, and the environments that these various social circles give aid in his multifaceted growth. Adolescents should get advice from their parents and teachers in selecting appropriate social circles. One could damage their job if the desire for companionship causes them to be blind to its true nature. Here, the roles of parents and teachers are essential.

Teachers and other adults the adolescent interact with can have a significant impact on their development. The peer group, however, has the biggest influence. Adolescents might even refuse to listen to their parents when they are neglecting their classmates; instead of losing their temper, parents should try to convince their children to see why, especially if the peer pressure led them to make a poor decision. Biological and cultural variables interact dialectically in human development, he emphasizes the significance of cultural factors—that is, the social environment—and contradicts Piaget's unbalanced developmental psychology.

Proper teaching techniques:

Due to the adolescent's high level of creativity and activity, the teaching-learning process would benefit from a creative approach; several activities should be introduced as tools for growth and learning.

The approach and tactics used should support the kid's natural process of cognitive development because this is the stage of development when the youngster becomes more argumentative and develops reasoning skills at the level of an adult.

The Heuristic technique, or question-answer method, should be used to actively involve the students in the construction of the lesson rather than spoon-feeding them ready-made answers. Students need to be given with issues so they may think critically and thoroughly in order to come up with solutions.

Such approaches would be very beneficial in further honing their logical faculties. Asking incisive questions will significantly improve your capacity for thought. A real-world problem may be presented, and by asking questions, it may be possible to extract a response that alone will solve the issue.

The question-and-answer format offers the most opportunities for class involvement. A proper state of group dynamism emerges. According to Wright HF and his colleagues, 70% of the things that happen to a child at school are brought about by interactions that happen there every day as a result of various activities.

The teaching approach should be such that it provides the greatest number of opportunities for interaction and that it organizes these interactions into extremely helpful repertoires of experiences to draw upon when learning new things.

The project-method is another excellent teaching strategy for teenagers. It would offer sufficient opportunities for creativity where the best learning occurs through doing and the students are actively engaged with one another.

The disposition and requirements of the adolescent would be best served by a discovery or inquiry approach. He ought to be able to identify the issue. The environment should permit the student to conduct research freely and appropriately.

It should be possible for the discoverer to access all necessary physical resources. The teacher's function should be that of a facilitator, assisting the student in moving forward and toward the goal. The teacher should observe carefully and only intervene if he or she believes that the students are about to veer off course.

First-hand knowledge gained from direct observation tends to be more distinct and persistent. A teenager may also like nothing more than going on trips and excursions to study. The youth should be taken on outings to zoos, museums, exhibitions, and other places; as well as to industries, banks, and post offices to show them how things work.

The empirical approach, stated that learning by doing is a very essential principle. This would show to be a very successful guiding idea for educating adolescents.

And the most crucial thing the school should do is to offer strong sources of inspiration so that students can continue to work hard to mimic. Adolescents daydream, and someone or something usually captures their attention as a hero.

It is the responsibility of teachers to give such role models to their students in order to motivate them to grow into the ideal personality types.

The last but not least requirement for the teenage student is a sympathetic teacher who understands the pressure an adolescent is working under—he or she is confused because of rapid spurts in bodily changes, powerful onsets of sexual impulses, and emotional disturbances, among other things.

For them, the teacher should act as a very reliable counselor. He ought to act in a friendly and motivating manner. He should have the traits of a learned educator with a strong moral code so that he can serve as a role model for the students to follow.

The adolescent would either become irritable and neurotic or may become a delinquent if the parents are strict and the teacher is insane.

Chapter 9

STAGES OF A CHILD DEVELOPMENT AND PSYCHOLOGY

Physical Development

Most 13 to 17-year-old teenagers will;

Begin to change physically from childhood gradually into maturity, and then full-blown puberty.

Females particularly, will almost reach adult height (males continue to grow taller into their early twenties.)

Brain/Cognitive Development

Most 13 to 17-year-old youths will:

Become cognitively mature, which is the capacity to decide based on awareness of possibilities and their effects.

Continue to let peers influence you (The power of peer pressure lessens after early adolescence.)

Develop the abilities you need to be independent

Respond to media messages while honing your capacity to examine them

Increase the level of maturity in interactions with family and friends.

Aspire to have more control on their own lives

Learn to drive and become more independent

Development Of Emotions

Most 13 to 17-year-old youths will:

Have the ability to create long-lasting, mutually beneficial relationships provided they have the necessary elements in place, such as trust, a happy past, and an appreciation for love.

Understanding their own feelings and the capacity to consider the reasons behind them.

Progressively start to appreciate personality more than appearance

Sexual Development

Most 13 to 17-year-old youths will:

Recognize their sexuality, comprehend their possibilities for expressing it, and are aware of the negative effects of doing so. They choose to express their sexuality in ways that may or may not involve engaging in shared sexual behaviors.

Recognize what makes relationships good or harmful.

Understand pregnancy, HIV, and other sexually transmitted diseases in detail.

Recognize how various media influence how society views sex and have the potential to learn about close, enduring relationships.

To be aware of one's own sexual orientation (This is different than sexual behavior)

Chapter 10

HOW FAMILIES CAN RAISE SEXUALLY HEALTHY TEENS

Your family's and religion's stances on sexual activity should be made clear. Make it clear that even if having sex is fun, young people should wait to start it until they are in a committed, enduring relationship.

Describe the various ways that each of us can show our love and experience intimacy.

Talk with your teen about the aspects that you both believe should be taken into consideration when making decisions about having sex, such as age, consent from both parties, protection, the use of contraceptives, love, intimacy, etc.

Encourage teens to make decisions while giving them facts to base their decisions on.

Talk about several forms of contraception and emphasize the value of using condoms.

Talk to them about their alternatives, such as emergency contraception, STI testing, and treatment, should unprotected sexual activity occur. If a teen becomes pregnant, talk about her or his alternatives, such as adoption, parenting, and abortion.

Talk about why exploitative behavior is unhealthy and, in some situations, illegal.

Help young people recognize different verbal and physical reactions to avoid/leave uncomfortable sexual situations.

Recognize that youth have a variety of options for their future, some of which include marriage and/or parenthood while others may elect to remain single and/or childless.

Use language that is inclusive and acknowledges that some young people may be gay, lesbian, bisexual, or transgender.

DISCUSSIONS RELATING TO GROWTH

Some parents may find it challenging to start conversations regarding their children's growth, development, and sexuality since they themselves did not grow up in a setting where such topics were covered. Some parents might worry that they don't have the right answers or be unsure of how much information to give. Think about these advices to assist:

First, promote communication by ensuring your kids that they are free to discuss anything with you.

Make the most of teaching opportunities. A conversation can be started by a friend's pregnancy, a news story, or a TV program.

Instead of talking, listen more.

Consider what is being asked of you. Verify with your child that what you heard matches the question they intended to ask.

Don't make snap judgments. An adolescent asking about sex does not necessarily mean they are having or considering having sex.

Respond to inquiries succinctly and directly. Give answers that are accurate, sincere, succinct, and straightforward.

Observe your child's opinions. Help your youngster share their opinions and ideals while also sharing your own.

Reassure young kids that their inquiries and thoughts are normal, just as they are.

Give your kids advice on how to avoid dangerous situations and how to make wise sex decisions.

Recognize your ignorance of a question's response. Suggest that the two of you jointly research the solution online or in a library.

Mention how your adolescent might occasionally find it easier to chat to someone else than you. Consider other dependable adults who they can speak to.

www.ingramcontent.com/pod-product-compliance
Lightning Source LLC
Chambersburg PA
CBHW061555250726
48657CB00021B/1813